D1489443

What's Wrong?
IN THE WILD

Catherine Veitch
Illustrated by Fermin Solis

Quarto is the authority on a wide range of topics.

Quarto educates, entertains and enriches the lives of our readers—enthusiasts and lovers of hands-on living.

www.quartoknows.com

Author: Catherine Veitch
Illustrator: Fermin Solis
Designer: Victoria Kimonidou
Editor: Emily Pither

© 2018 Quarto Publishing plc

First Published in 2018 by QEB Publishing,
an imprint of The Quarto Group.
6 Orchard Road
Suite 100
Lake Forest, CA 92630
T: +1 949 380 7510
F: +1 949 380 7575
www.QuartoKnows.com

All rights reserved. No part of this publication may be reproduced, stored in a retrieval system, or transmitted in any form or by any means, electronic, mechanical, photocopying, recording, or otherwise, without the prior permission of the publisher, nor be otherwise circulated in any form of binding or cover other than that in which it is published and without a similar condition being imposed on the subsequent purchaser.

A CIP record for this book is available from the Library of Congress.

ISBN 978 1 68297 373 8

Manufactured in Dongguan, China TL042018

9 8 7 6 5 4 3 2 1

FSC
www.fsc.org

MIX
Paper from
responsible sources
FSC® C104723

WHAT'S WRONG IN THE WILD?

Hi, we're Leah and Eddie! Join us as we travel the world and discover all sorts of interesting animals.

But watch out! In each scene there are **five** out of place things to spot.

Can you find them all? Look carefully, as some are hard to spot. Turn to the back of the book for handy explanations about what's wrong, as well as a **strange but true!** fact per scene—these might seem wrong, but they're actually right!

LET THE SEARCH BEGIN!

CONTENTS

SAVANNA

It's thirsty work in the hot, dry savanna! It doesn't rain much here, so it's great to find a waterhole like this. Try to spot **five things** that are wrong or don't belong here. Can you say what's wrong with them or where they do belong? There are **two clues** to help you.

There's a creature here there that looks like a woolly elephant, but isn't alive today.

There's an animal in the water that doesn't belong here! Its name rhymes with *park*.

5

RAINFOREST

It's hot, steamy, and sticky in the rainforest. There are multicolored frogs, fish with teeth, color-changing chameleons, and spiders as big as plates! Can you spot **five things** that are wrong or don't belong here? There are **two clues** to help you.

ARCTIC

The Arctic is one of the coldest and iciest places on our planet. Wrap up warm as it's a ch-ch-chilly −4°F in the Arctic today. Can you find the **five things** that are wrong or don't belong here? Can you say what's wrong with them or where they do belong? There are **two clues** to help.

HO

One of those bears
doesn't belong here!
Its name begins
with a "p."

Those greedy bears
over there are in
a sticky mess!

DESERT

Deserts can reach a scorching 115°F. Don't stay out in the hot sun for too long and there's no time to build sandcastles! Many creatures however have adapted to survive in this heat. Can you spot **five things** that are wrong or don't belong here? There are **two clues** to help.

There's something bumpy about one of those camels.

Dung beetles usually roll something much smellier!

11

FOREST

It's easy to get lost in this huge forest, but Leah and Eddie are safe on the cycle path. There are lots of cozy places for animals to make their homes here. Try to find **five things** that are wrong or don't belong here. Can you say what's wrong with them or where they do belong? There are **two clues** to help.

FARM

Pull on your galoshes and squelch in the mud. There's lots of work to do on a farm. There are animals to feed and clean, eggs to collect, and cows to milk. Try to find the **five things** that are wrong or don't belong here. There are **two clues** to help.

OCEAN

Beautiful creatures live in the warm, shallow water around a coral reef. Dive in and take a look. Be careful not to break the coral as it takes thousands of years to grow. Try to spot **five things** that are wrong or don't belong here. Can you say what's wrong with them or where they do belong? There are **two clues** to help you.

UNDERGROUND

Shovel, scuttle, scratch...there's a lot going on under our feet. Many animals are busy digging burrows. Some live in them, and others use them to escape from predators. Try to spot **five things** that are wrong or don't belong here. Can you say what's wrong with them or where they do belong? There are **two clues** to help.

One of these animals is doing something strange. Its name rhymes with *hole.*

This animal has lots of feet, but something isn't quite right with them!

19

IN THE AIR

Fly up, up, up, and away, as high as a bird. But hold on tight because it's windy! What can you see? Try to spot **five things** that are wrong or don't belong here. Can you say what's wrong with them or where they do belong? There are **two clues** to help.

ANSWERS

SAVANNA

These **five things** are wrong in the picture:

(1) Giraffes don't drink from glasses! They get most of their water from the plants they eat.

(2) Zebras have black and white stripes, so this zebra is wrong.

(3) Lions don't like vegetables! They are meat-eaters and hunt animals such as zebras, antelopes, buffaloes, and giraffes.

(4) Sharks don't belong in the savanna! They live in oceans.

(5) Woolly mammoths lived thousands of years ago. We know about them from pictures people drew on cave walls in the past.

⭐ **Strange but true!** Giraffes spread out their front legs to help them bend down and drink water, because otherwise, they're too tall to reach!

RAINFOREST

(1) Piranhas don't wear glasses! They have a great sense of smell so they will sniff you before they see you anyway!

(2) It might rain a lot in the rainforest, but monkeys don't use umbrellas!

(3) Kangaroos live in grassy parts of Australia and Tasmania where they can munch on mouthwatering grass.

(4) This sloth might look sweet, but sloths are folivores and eat leaves, not cakes!

(5) Monkeys love to swing through the trees, but use their limbs and tail to help them. There aren't playground swings in the rainforest!

⭐ **Strange but true!** Chameleons can change the color of their skin to show how they are feeling, or to hide in their surroundings.

These **five things** are wrong in the picture:

ARCTIC

(1) This poor puss wouldn't survive for long in the freezing Arctic, and would struggle to pull a heavy sled.

(2) These sassy polar bears don't eat honey in the wild. They mostly hunt seals for food.

(3) Arctic puffins don't eat hot dogs! They snack on fish that they catch.

(4) Seals don't need inflatable rings to swim! They use their big, strong flippers to steer through the water.

(5) This poor panda is lost. Pandas live in China where they can feast on bamboo

⭐ **Strange but true!** This might look like a whale with a unicorn horn, but it's a type of whale called a narwhal. Its tusk can grow up to 10 feet (3 m) long!

These **five things** are wrong in the picture:

DESERT

1. This camel has a few too many humps! Dromedary or Arabian camels have one hump and Bactrian camels have two.

2. Dung beetles don't play soccer! But they do roll balls of poop along the ground. They lay their eggs in the dung and their babies eat it. Yuk!

3. The armadillo's hard skin looks like armor, but it doesn't wear a helmet with feathers! An armadillo's tough skin protects it from predators.

4. A desert tortoise has a shell on its back—not a house! It makes a cozy home in burrows underground.

5. Desert bighorn sheep don't need to wear sunglasses or sunhats. They are expert mountain climbers and rest in shady spots among the rocks.

★ **Strange but true!** This creature looks like a mouse-sized kangaroo with enormous ears—but it's actually a rodent called a long-eared jerboa.

These **five things** are wrong in the picture:

FOREST

1. Noisy woodpeckers do hammer trees, but they don't use a hammer! They use their beaks to break up the bark and find insects hiding underneath.

2. Lots of rabbits live in forests, but they don't wear top hats!

3. Squirrels don't eat ice cream! They snack on nuts, acorns, and insects.

4. A fox can't play the trumpet. But foxes can make lots of other sounds. For example, they can howl, growl, purr, bark, or whine.

5. The pterodactyl lived millions of years ago and isn't alive today, so you wouldn't find one flying in a forest.

★ **Strange but true!** This raccoon isn't wearing a bandit's mask! Raccoons have an area of black fur around their eyes.

These **five things** are wrong in the picture:

FARM

1. A very strange hen would have laid this egg—it's multicolored and striped!

2. Roosters can't play the guitar, but they do make a lot of noise when they crow in the morning!

3. Ducks don't wear galoshes! But their wide, webbed feet do protect them in puddles by stopping them from slipping on the wet ground.

4. Tigers don't live on farms! Most live in forests, rainforests, or mountains.

5. Rats don't play cards! But young rascal rats do like to play by chasing and jumping on each other.

★ **Strange but true!** This isn't a person in a field, it's a scarecrow—clothes on a stick made to look like a person! Farmers use these to stop birds from eating crops.

These **five things** are wrong in the picture:

OCEAN

1. Sharks don't wear bow ties and have curly mustaches! Although some fish do have "whiskers" near the mouth that can be used to search for food.

2. Clownfish may be funny, but they can't juggle! They use their fins for swimming and not for juggling.

3. Lobsters don't eat with a knife and fork! They use their strong claws to break open hard shells so they can eat the soft creature inside.

4. A sea turtle doesn't need a snorkel and plastic flippers! It has its own two strong front flippers that it pushes through the water to swim fast.

5. Dogs can't breathe underwater. Although, there is a style of swimming called doggy paddling!

★ **Strange but true!** This shark really does have a head shaped like a hammer —it's called a hammerhead shark and it has eyes at the side of its head.

These **five things** are wrong in the picture:

UNDERGROUND

1. Some centipedes have over a hundred feet, but they don't wear socks. That would be a lot of socks!

2. Moles are good at digging, but they don't use shovels to dig. They have strong front legs and long claws for digging tunnels underground.

3. This poor budgie is a long way from home. Budgerigars in the wild nest in trees and don't live underground.

4. Badgers don't listen to music! A badger has good hearing and listens out for danger, or small animals and insects that it can eat.

5. Rats aren't green! They're usually brown, gray, or black and their color camouflages them in the soil.

★ **Strange but true!** This ant may be small, but it's strong enough to carry that big leaf! A single ant can carry at least 10 times its own body weight.

These **five things** are wrong in the picture:

IN THE AIR

1. This nest looks a bit overcrowded! The penguin shouldn't be in this nest as penguins can't fly, so it wouldn't live high up in the trees.

2. Birds use their wings to fly—they don't use parachutes!

3. There's no such thing as a duck astronaut! But animals have been to space before. In 1957 a Russian dog named Laika was sent into space.

4. Owls don't need glasses! But they do have to turn their heads to look to the side because they can't move their eyes sideways like we can.

5. Birds don't build their nests from popcorn! They use twigs, and put soft things like grass and moss inside to make their nests comfy.

★ **Strange but true!** This squirrel belongs in the air! Flying squirrels don't actually fly, they glide—the skin between their paws acts like a parachute.

These **five things** are wrong in the picture: